Interactive Press

How to Measure the Distance of Things

Paul Whitby is a casual animal rescuer and poet. His writing has been published in journals such as *Cordite*, *The Lifted Brow*, and *Offset*. He won the Ipswich Poetry Prize in 2021, and the Wyndham Writing Award the following year. His first book of poetry, *Rats Live on no Evil Star*, was published in 2013, and he won the Malthouse Theatre Award for Excellence in Creative Arts later that year.

Previously a house sitter, Paul currently resides in Yarrambat, Victoria.

Interactive Press
Brisbane

How to Measure the Distance of Things

Paul Whitby

Interactive Press

Interactive Press
an imprint of IP (Interactive Publications Pty Ltd)
Treetop Studio • 9 Kuhler Court
Carindale, Queensland, Australia 4152
sales@ipoz.biz
http://ipoz.biz/

Printed in 12 pt Adobe Caslon Pro on 14 pt Avenir Book.

ISBN: 978192830494 (PB); 978192830500 (eBk)

A catalogue record for this
book is available from the
National Library of Australia

Acknowledgements

Book design: David P Reiter
Cover image: Ben Pobje
Author photo: Ben Fletcher

Three poems in this book have been previously published. "Superproduct" appeared in *Sacred/Profane*, "It is Written" was published in *Offset*, then later appeared in *Award Winning Australian Poems*. "Common Burn" was published in *Wyndham Writing Awards Anthology*.

I wish to express gratitude to my friend and mentor Andy Jackson for his patience and support. I would also like to thank Claire Gaskin for her line edits and sense of humour. Special thanks go out to Bronwen Manger and Gemma White for reading my manuscript, and for their belief in my work. My deepest gratitude goes out to them for their unwavering friendship and support.

Contents

I

Ambulance

The sky is blue
and the trees are green.
I reckon it's about 1:30.

Outside people
are crashing their cars,
boarding trains.
I'm not saying anything,
but still.

A good person
never forgives himself.
Is that an ambulance,
or is it the reincarnated
being reinstated?

Cows chew grass,
birds fall from the sky.
I wait at the desk
for something to happen.

Dog God

Dogs are, in the basic sense,
the exact shape of everything
that was taken from us –
as if the God of our image
pressed a dog-shaped cookie cutter
down on our doughy hearts.

There was a younger time
when we belonged to the world,
and dog was god and god was dog,
and we saw that it was good.
We waded through weeds
and muddied our clothes.

But we got too big for ourselves,
and the bigger became the small.

And Dog God didst evict
our sorry arses from Eden,
and as a parting gift
gave us a constant companion
to remind us of everything
we are and will never be.

And we watch and smile
as they jump into the lake
and chase the ducks into the sky.
For we still know how they feel
as we stand by, arms crossed
recalling another life.

Hugo

She doesn't want to see Hugo.
She doesn't even know she doesn't
but I do and she doesn't.
I tell her, "You'll like it.
It'll appeal to your inner child."

But for reasons couched inside
those squelchy pink hemispheres,
she doesn't want to see it.
She'll resist Hugo with silence
until one of us finally dies.

I can't know, but I suspect
it's because it's a boy's fantasy.
Or maybe the title annoys her:
too Frenchy, too cliched?
Some schmaltzy kind of shit.

That's what my mind thinks
her mind is thinking,
if she's thinking about it at all.
She's probably thinking about
a choc-top ice cream.

A year comes and goes.
Hugo's probably all scratched up
in the weekly loans section.
We're now halfway through
season three of *True Blood*.

It's a chick thing, really:
slightly sado-masochistic,
money shots in blood.
Hugo seems far away now.
I guess this must be love.

Inside Cat

It's a cold winter's day.
I'm at my parents' house,
alone in front of the fire,
listening to the cat
eating her arsehole out.

I'm minding the place
while the olds are up north
at Gemini Resort.
I can't complain, I guess,
it's got all the comforts.

On still mornings like this,
the fog gives the trees
a ghostly presence.
I couldn't say the time,
or even what day it is.

I have nowhere to be,
there's nothing I have to do.
Centrelink lost interest
years ago. I got my wish:
I've been written off.

No-one depends on me
except the cat, and to her
I am everything.
If she could open my mouth
and climb in, she would.

She became an inside cat
a few years back,
and spent all her time
loitering near the door
hoping to escape.

Her existential meows
were harrowing.

Now, if she sees a bird
near the window,
it doesn't even register.
Everything is equal
in its lack of value.

All she has is my lap
and her arsehole.

But she gurgles and slurps
and makes a meal of it,
while I sit here and listen
to each lap of her tongue
marking the time.

Canary Found

I found a canary today.
This is not a poem.

He was canary yellow
& he sang
like a bird.

He still is –
canary yellow, I mean.
Still sings, too.

Well not *right now*,
I mean in the mornings
When I open the blinds.

I'm not being funny.
Every word is true!

I didn't find the canary.
He was there
to be found.

He was hanging around
outside a house.

He wasn't hanging.
He was bouncing along
on the pavement.

(why is language
so draining?)

I rang the doorbell
and he flew to the porch
but no-one answered.

Then other stuff happened.
          Went home
          Got a blanket
          Came back
          Threw it over him
          Brought him home

This is not a poem.
You don't need the details.

I made fliers, did a
CANARY FOUND
leaflet drop.

It's three weeks now
since I found a canary.

I did not find the canary.
The canary found me.

This is not a poem.
A poem is not a canary.

Mental Health Trip: Falls Creek

When they first put me on skis,
I fell over. So they bound my feet
tighter, adjusted a few straps,
and clipped me back in. I fell over
again.

Now they've faced me uphill,
in the grooves of the other skiers.
I watch our group struggling ahead,
like frogs that have learned
to walk upright. I inch forward.

When I fall again, I don't try
to get up. The new worker says,
"Paul, why aren't you getting up?
You've got to get up; the rest
are getting too far ahead. Paul?"

He radios through, "Something's
wrong: Paul won't talk to me."

Dead Bodies

I've never seen a dead body.
There was a cadaver
on the tracks one day,
near where I was living.
There was a sheet over it,
but I did see the feet.
It was a long time ago.

I was talking to a friend
who said that her Dad
had an open coffin,
and when she looked in
he seemed to wink at her –
which made sense because
it was the sort of thing
that he used to do.
She asked her son later on,
but he said, "I was busy
watching him breathe."

When I see a dead body
for the first time, it should
be someone close to me.
Perhaps I'll touch the body,
so I know how it feels –
but I'm really not sure.

I imagine the body laid out.
It shines as I approach,
as if it has been waiting
a long time for me to arrive.

It is Written

It's midnight. You're washing dishes
for the third time today;
touching the sharp point of nothing.
A pathetic breeze leaks
through the window, crickets grate.

You've been watching TV all night.
Documentaries – *Death
of the Coorong, The Exxon-Valdiz*
and *Men who have Sex
with Blow-up Dolls.* Then

when you switch off,
you sit in the dark, head going
into noughts and crosses.
There is a world inside you.
It is over-populated, and

things are dire. Millions cry out
in tongues you do not understand.
And so here you are,
sweating into the sink,
cleaning it all away. Later

you will go outside, with the air
hanging down on you like a wet towel.
You will throw your food scraps
onto the lawn. They will be gone
by morning, to God knows where.

And there you will stand.
In the outside lights, your shadow
will cast many angles.

Do not be afraid. All we need
is for you to give us the word.
Because no matter what you claim,
or disown, a poem will be written,
and it will be in your hand.

Lake Wyngala, Near Cowra, off the A41

I'm alone and in the dark,
walking along the shore of a dam,
tripping over things that were
submerged. There's a fierce wind,
and I hear waves crashing
on the black shores.

I keep thinking,
one of these days, dude,
you'll break a leg,
you'll fall down a mine shaft,
or into an open sewer,
because, why not? Snakebite,
now there's one that I dread.
Had a Red-Bellied Black
cross my path the other day,
which is an eternity of bad luck
if you get bitten and die.
Now things have gotten sandy,
and I smush along.
I walk towards a dejected light.
I'll be home tomorrow,
to Melbourne, where I know
every indifference by sight.
Poetry screams at me,
Infinite stars and a deafening roar.

And what do you know,
it's a Telstra Payphone.
Always there when you need it.
I pick up the receiver
and say, "Are you there?"

It's abominable, describing
what is real and alive,
to contrive the world like this.
Something passes through me,
and I am left here
with my smallness and tiny ideas.
Whatever you are, I'm sorry,
but you speak another language,
and I've taken to talking to myself.

Alluvial Nugget

The best shit I ever had was a crazy shit.
It happened around the time I was diagnosed;
I was so wound up I couldn't be around people,
and I hadn't even thought about crapping for days.
Then I went for a lockdown-breaking walk
through the ruins of gold-rush Panton Hill.
The mood started to lift, and poetry soared.
I saw dragonflies gleam, the blooming wattle
overwhelmed me with love – and I realised,
I just had to take a shit.

There was a small alluvial dig nearby,
and I squatted, and sunshine beamed from my arse.
I looked down in wonder at my perfect poo.
I didn't want to move on, but a blowfly
began to show some interest.
I buried my newborn in a shallow grave
of dried leaves, and like the pioneers,
I carried on, beside the flooded creek,
the cicadas making the air shimmer,
knowing I'd left the best of myself behind.

Exhumed Poem

Come with us now on a journey
through time and space...
– The Mighty Boosh

My poems link hands
across the space-time hooey.

I'm at Coburg Lake
crying beside my rat's grave.
On the walk home
I write half a poem,
then I bury it deep.

Ten years later I finish it
and publish it as Paul South.

I gather the words together
as if they were mine –
it's a common language,
my vocab could be bigger.
What're you gonna do?

Each moment's just another
one-liner.

In the morning, newness
abounds around the place.
Birds do somersaults in the trees.
I find an old version of me
half-baked in the oven –

something I left for another
time.

Autobiography

after Lawrence Ferlinghetti

I am eighteen years old.
I'm actually one hundred.
In my spare time
I like to argue with my girlfriend.

I am the last cigarette
in the packet these days.
I wash dishes, asleep by midnight,
up again, shave.

I prefer to avoid people
but I go insane if I do
so I show up again
like leftovers.

Sometimes I think
I've seen all there is to see
and know all I want to know
but then my girlfriend

explains to me
exactly how I'm full of shit
and I have to admit
she's probably onto something.

I have shelves of books
offering sage advice.
I can't bring myself
to read a word.

I am happiest on my feet,
I like waterbirds – ducks, geese,
I eat a spinach roll,
I laugh during sex.

I am and I continue
away from conception,
and I can't stop pushing,
I'm giving birth to myself.

Pillow Talk

I was lying on the bed
after a wank and a shower,
listening to Eno,
and I had my right arm
outstretched.

I turned to my hand and said,
"Was it good for you?"
Then I made a mouth-shape
with my hand, and said,
"It was wonderful, darling."

And then I laughed
like I was completely insane.
I haven't laughed like that
since the good times
when we were together.

Coke

You don't get to drink coke at home.
You ask why, of course. They never answer
to your satisfaction. But when you grow older,
you understand: it was the 1970s,
and your parents were concerned and informed.
Coke, back then, was the next wave
of invasion – like Prickly Pear, Cane Toads
– an ugly thing.

In the school portable, there's a row of jars
along the windowsills, full of cola,
and in the bottom of each jar is a child's tooth.
You look across at your jar and wonder.
In the late afternoon, the sun catches the glass.
The contents glows, and you imagine
you are looking up from the bottom of a lake.
Mrs. Brown encourages the class
to go over and examine their tooth,
but the students lose interest in a week or two.

But you don't lose interest in Coke.
Like that sweet tooth in the jar, it remains,
tarnished perhaps, but catching the light.

And then, once in a while, you're handed over
to the care of a friend's family. Your thoughts
are so quiet that you can hardly hear them.
And you're given a bottle by some young mother,
not the real coke, but a syrupy mix,
like Slade's, or Gold Medal.

You feel its weight in your hand, a substance hard-won.
And, as you pour it down your throat,
you can feel the corrosion happening inside you,
the first steps towards wanting,
long summer holidays, standing at the shore,
the tide fizzing backwards, tugging at your feet.

The Beast

It's everything I expected and worse.
And everyone knows a guy:
It's the head gasket.
The radiator's fucked.
What you've got there
            is a cracked engine block.

I look at their faces,
try to decide who's straight up.

I took it to the mechanic
that I bought it from, a nice guy,
a devout Muslim.

Days passed.
Went in to see what was going on.
There was no-one around so
I went out into the back yard.
Behind the rusting wrecks
was a herd of floppy-eared goats.

I knelt down, hand extended
with an offering of grass;
the goats just stared and baa-ed.
Then a young mechanic came out.
I'd never seen him before.

"It's bad news," he said.
"Huh?" I got up and rubbed my knees.
"The engine, it's the engine."
"The engine?" I said.

I looked to the goats.
The goats looked back.

"You have a problem with your engine."
"What kind of problem?"
He smiled. "A big problem."
He held out a spark plug.
"See this spark plug? Rusty," he said.
"Mm."

Clearly I wasn't impressed enough.
"It should look like this," he said,
and brandished a sparkling clean plug.
There was a pause for emphasis.
"Water is leaking into the head gasket."
"Oh," I said. "Baa," said the goats.

"Well...what should I do?"
He gestured skywards with his hands.
"Impossible to know," he said,
then added, "maybe buy another car?"

The goats retreated behind the wrecks;
a cloud passed over the sun.
"I don't have money for another car."
He was philosophical.
"You want to fix, we will fix
for you – no problem. For you
a good car maybe, who knows?"

"You'll fix it for me? For free?"
He laughed. "Heavens, no!
This will cost THOUSANDS!"
"Why do you have the goats?" I asked.
"Festival!"

Superproduct

Sweeping the world like a pandemic
Felching the poorest corners of Bollywood
Free in packs of Cornflakes
For a limited time
Collect all 30 and win a Ferrari
Free radical baseball caps for the kids
Just SMS 'tumour' for your
Cancer like a horse's cock
Trembling through power grids
Fizzing overhead wires
Viral load to shut down web browsers
Nikkei going into noughts and crosses
Burns porn upon retinas
Rips bukkake like a haiku
Converts money into euros
Speaks Esperanto with pan American accent
Moves into the Kardashian house
Has a threesome with god and the devil
Watch now for $5.95/min
Turns swamps into satellite suburbs
Fucks your default page settings
Photoshops behinds breasts
Voice modulates Guy Sebastian
Pulps and reincarnates as phrases
heard on mobile phones on trains

Tense

When she is dead
she eats bracken for breakfast
she takes up Sudoku
to kill the millennia
her words are written in stone
and that suits her fine

When she is alive
she complains about adverts
Big Brother and *MasterChef*
but she won't stop watching
she locks the doors at dusk
when she's alive

Now she's dead again
at least I think so because
the trees dance about
like zombie cheerleaders
and she doesn't have much
of any substance to say

I woke up from a fever
the frogs talking of sunset
I crept out barefooted
up the hall towards the TV
a galaxy of star-power
she was basking in the glow

I watch her switch
between life and death now.
It's speeding up until

I'm not sure which is who
sunrise and sunset
the chicken and the egg

Later when I'm dead
and everyone is dead
I say *Remember that night*
I came to you and said
I was afraid of you dying?
And again you say nothing

Babies

Babies are a thing
that happens to other people,
the kind of event
you read about on facebook,
like a volcano vomiting
on domestic homes,
burying people alive.

I don't hate babies,
they're just a fact of nature.
And there is a beauty I guess
in a mudslide, the way
it flows into the valley
and cakes the boulders.
If people are into that,
it's nothing to do with me.

I certainly don't blame
babies for being born,
any more than I do a tornado
for ripping through homes,
tossing everything about.
It's really not personal to me.
Babies are just a thing.

Swarm

It was years ago, in high summer,
one of those evenings when the heat
lifts the veil after long days of
something else.
The smell of cool earth led me
to step outside of the house.
I picked my way
along a path between two houses,
to the creek behind the estate.

Through the tangle of scrub,
the sky looked bloody.
There was no sound,
nothing left to feel, but
that air against my skin.

I walked behind the old school,
around the back of the oval.
My feet seemed to walk
entirely above the ground.

Across the oval was a lamp-post;
it was lit up just enough
to see how dark it was getting.
I padded across the oval.

At the base of the pole
were puddles of angry colour,
a kind of shimmering.
I came closer and saw
it was a mass of winged ants.

They wriggled and flipped
on their backs, legs kicking.

I jumped on the ants
with all the weight of a child.
I didn't know why I was doing it,
but the heat made it good.
I crushed all that I could.

Common Burn

A.D.H.D. is an absence
held so close
that you wouldn't recognise
yourself or the world
if it was gone.

Sometimes it's a wrestle,
but usually an embrace.

For example, I am driving
the Emerald-Monbulk Rd.
It's a warm summer's night.
'Common Burn' by Mazzy Star,
the vibraphone chimes
shimmer through the car.
I stray the way clouds do,
across the road looking up
at the sky, a bowl of water.

And I feel the world
experiencing itself through me.

I'm present to little things.
It's hard to be close to me
sometimes. I had a friend
and he was telling me
about something
to do with breaking up
with his girlfriend.
It was hard to see her.
She worked in the deli and

he was in produce,
I think, but a sparrow
lands on the table behind him
and begins picking at
the scrambled eggs.

She wasn't replying
to his text messages
and the sparrow is so close
I notice the subtle layers
and the shades of brown
upon his wings.
And he was despairing,
but then she hadn't returned
the engagement ring.
So, you know.

Wherever I am now,
I'm somewhere else.
The train doors shut
and I watch my backpack
glide by on the seat,
teacher throws a duster
at my head and the kids
        laugh at me.

I can't say where I'm going,
but when I'm driving
through the forest like this,
I find I'm not too worried
about the trees.

II

House Sitter

the uncanny
self-revealing pain of
a slow melody
as it walks through time
takes your hand
for a while
and leaves you crying
waiting on a bagel

put on your sunnies
so the waiter
won't see into your soul
you wanted
a toasted sandwich
but just couldn't
bring yourself to say
"toastie"
to the only person
you'll talk to today

silent on Facebook
swiping through memes
and country town bitching
it isn't your real name –
Paul South –
you use it so no exes
or family will find you

'Healesville's smoky
and not from a pizza oven
a holiday setting

without the holiday
empty houses
lonely cats barking dogs
you're a prize a boon
to retirees now
widows hand you the keys
a glint in their eyes
middle age lends you
a credibility
you don't understand

Mental Health Trip: The Bus

- Do you know John Denver?
- No.
- Do you know Glen Campbell, then?
- Ah, I think I know one of his songs.
- You know John Denver,
the guy who died in helicopter crash.
- Nah.
- Anyway, I like Glen Campbell.
You know that song about the trees?
And that river – something something...
travelling... yeah that's it. Travelling on.
- I know 'Rhinestone Cowboy'.
- Oh yeah, I know that one too.
- John Denver, you know, died
in a helicopter crash. Tragic waste.
- Oh well, I guess we all got to die.
- Yeah, but not in a helicopter crash!
- No, yeah, no, I see what you mean.
- When I die, the only way I want to
be buried is in a bathtub in the ground.
No fuss, just a bathtub –
you know, so nothing can get in.

Getting There

He comes in from weeding
around the roses and looks at me.
He pours a glass of orange juice.
"Getting there," he says,
and I say, "Getting where?"
But he just gulps down his drink,
and then gets on with it.

Now he's out on the front lawn.
"Look what he's doing," says Mum,
watching from the window.
We watch him picking up gumnuts.
"Silly old man, the next breath
of wind and they're back again."
Mum and I are having a cuppa
when he comes back in again.

He's stripped to his singlet now.
"How many gumnuts did I pick up,
d'you reckon?" he says,
and wipes his face with a hanky.
Mum looks at me, and I shrug.
"I couldn't possibly guess."
"Three hundred and three," he says.
Then he walks over to the sink.

"You're too old for this," says Mum.
Dad finishes his water, gasps,
and then bangs the glass down.
"I picked up six buckets of twigs
and leaves too. Getting there."

Every day we're getting there.
Dad and I wash dishes together,
our dinner is almost cooked.
I try to fight it – I take long walks
along the river, going nowhere.
But I'm following this thread.

He was a marathon runner
when he was a younger man.
He would run for hours a day,
in training for the next race.
I was just a boy back then,
when he taught me how to run.

Night Light

I'm up late
and while you sleep until tomorrow
I think about the quiet sex we had
and how pitiful an orgasm can feel
at One a.m. on a Tuesday night

I'm eating Sultana Bran
mixed with All Bran and Zymil milk
and watching a YouTube clip
of Laurie Anderson talking
about Lou Reed and her talking
about life and love
and death and everything

and I'm aware of our age gap
and I wonder what will not be said
this time around or maybe ever
what we can give to each other
and will anybody really care
how many YouTube hits are enough
to keep something alive
and all I can think about is death

Later I will go to bed to find you
splayed out like roadkill
between us in the dark so many dreams
murky as the past and future

You have to be the future for me
I will keep the light burning
through the long cold hours

Late Riser

Throw a tarp over your dreams
wake up to yourself
you need to buy an iPhone
you've got to brush your tongue
laxatives and vitamins

There's a divine need
for you to get carried away
like this

Wake up to yourself
you've got a cat on your face
no time for a prayer
have a bowl of bracken and milk
peruse the to-do list
see out the window
kangaroos nibble away the time
mountains pale
before the summer

Start the car
it's a drive to the burbs
a printer cartridge
for your creativity
a smart phone holder
for the dash

Got to get moving
so you can beat the traffic

If you pass
a bend in the river
where trees hang their heads
for god's sake
don't look

For I Will Consider My Mother

after Mary Oliver

For I will consider my mother
For she takes consideration
For she moans like a ghost and already haunts me
For she's mislaid her reading glasses
For she needs her wheat bag microwaved
For when I'm very late, she says,
        "I thought you were DEAD!"
For she watches *National Nine News*
For she does not like windy nights
For she is the queen of Probus meetings
For she has seen Jersey Boys four times
For she can sit in a chair all day
For the Darrell Lea Liquorice is always in reach
For she feels guilty as she eats
For she says, "Look at this gut, I'm disgusting."
For her toddlers' walk is hard to watch
For she teeters on the brink
For she fell in the kitchen
and cracked her pelvis
For she wasn't the worst company on morphine
For we watched a lot of TV
For re-runs of *Heartbeat* aren't so bad
For I introduced her to *Breaking Bad*,
and she became addicted
For she is propped up by pillows
For the cookie jar is always full
For all the things we've never said
For she is frightened by storms
For she is afraid of birds in flight
For she locks the doors when she's alone

For she pushed me onto the dance floor
at my Brother-in-law's 50th
For she wants me to get married
For she asks me to have a shave
For she nags Dad for new carpet
For she is particular about tea
– weak, one flat sugar, a dash of cold
For the pill organiser needs organising
For the secret cache of Tim Tams
For the languor and the dread
For she says, "be careful," when I'm leaving
For she describes every ache and pain
For she subsidises my laziness
For she buys me bedtime booties
For the possum jumpers she wriggles into
For the pink dressing gown and slippers
For her past is one that remembers me
For her bicuspid heart valve needed replacing
For the stitches down her chest
For the infection, the mini-stroke
For she looked small in that hospital bed
For the photo of her holding me in her arms
For we hold her under the arms and lift her
For deferred hope and despair
For she walked into my room
and caught me masturbating
For she caught me dozens of times
For she loves me with a fierce need
For the years I didn't see her
            a negative space surrounded me
For the years dying in our collective memories
For the God in her stars
For everything that lifts us, and every fall
For the slow walk to surrender
For she stands in the doorway waving goodbye

Doing the Work

There comes a time where
you have to be doing the work.
And by definition it's awkward.
The chair's not high enough,
there's clutter on the desk.
And there's always that doubt –
shouldn't you
be paying your fine instalments?
They're all overdue.
So is ringing your friends,
getting some exercise,
cooking those lentils.
You have a yearning
to dig your toes into some earth,
and lay in the sunshine.

But it comes to you, a lightbulb
in a dingy study – and you get dirty,
you smear the page with your mess,
looping and careless, a continuous line
drawn from your innards, your heart
taking no prisoners.

Half-way Home

I never knew I'd need so many people
– David Bowie

Imagine a hot night.
I walk past a sign
on Johnson Street, saying:
THE PALE ALE
EXPERIMENT
A cool green bottle
perspires gently.
I consider this,
not quite understanding
what it means to me.
But I'm running late
for the N.A. meeting,
and I hurry on.

At the bus stop,
the seat looks into a bar
full of sunset people –
middle aged, worn out
jeans, women with bangs.
Janis Joplin sings
a scorching blues
I've never heard before.

And I think, Maybe
I should ring my ex,
see if she wants
to come down here.
Because it's hot,
it's almost summer and

she works a job she hates,
and oblivion and
then the bus comes.

Walking down Wellington,
I see a few smokers
out front of the church.
One person is bundled
on the ground. I walk up.
She's an ancient woman.

She has a felt tiger's head
on top of her head.
As she turns toward me,
dirty tassels swing out
from either side of her face.

"I turned 57 the other day,"
she says in my direction.
"Oh yeah?" I say.
She looks at least 80.
"I never thought
I'd make it this far."
"Well, I'm glad you did,"
I say, "or I'd be talking
to myself right now."
I guess she sort of laughs.
She has no idea
how much I need her.

Everyone heads inside
at the same moment,
by some herd instinct.

A young guy is asked up.
"I feel like using today.
I don't know why –
I'm three years clean."

Next guy is much older.
He says, "I'm just feeling
so much gratitude.
My life is simple –
I work, I have a home.
It's strange. I never knew
what living meant."

While the basket
is being passed around,
the chair asks if there are
any newcomers.
Everyone claps
someone up the back.
I can't see him
until he is helped
to the front of the room.
He's perhaps 50,
using a walking frame.
He turns to face us.
Words won't come,
and then he starts to cry.
"I'm fucked," he says,
"I'm fucked…"
He apologises, and
he is helped down again.

The room
explodes with applause.

Afterwards, I walk back
to Vic Park Station.
The streetlamps
look like the sun does
when the fires are on.

I come here to see
all the people I have been,
and who I could become.
I take them all with me,
and by the time I realise
I didn't notice the pub,
I'm already halfway home.

The Missing

What can you do
when a missing person
becomes trees, lorikeets,
sun-showers, synapses,
reflexes, invisible and real,
muttered words on a tram,
a young couple watching you
with dread?

Where can you go
to hide your naked head?
All your sentences die
at the first syllable –
they belong to the missing,
along with unfinished poems,
lost keys, and everything
you forgot to do.

Where do you find yourself
when someone pulls the plug
on the sky, and the dishwater
swirls and swirls? You can't
make sense of such a thing.
We watched the sun
become a black hole together.

Rosebud

My mind conjures brick houses,
wide backstreets bathed in sunshine.
I see fresh slices of orange;
Auntie Flo's horn-rimmed glasses.

And of course there is Grandma.

We will call them Kodak Moments.
Got the albums to prove it.

Those photos have now become the truth.
I remember everyone with orange skin,
the sky pastel blue.

We were children, we lived for the future.
Soon we'll get a gelati,
soon we'll go to the beach.

Not long now.

"The Kingswood, Dad says,
it's been around the equator six times;
it has been to the moon!

I look out the window at the golden moon,
with its pale blue craters.
This is what is true.

Trivia Night

Panton Hill Pub.
Wooden floors, walls, tables.
A sickening glaze.
Nothing for vegos,
except roast without the meat.
Roast parsnip, roast potatoes
and a side of chips.
A plate full of white –
white people eating,
white trivia.
Hard to digest;
they've come here to win.
They're in the wrong place.

Women's Tears

A NEW TONIC
FOR ALL THAT AILS:
WOMEN'S TEARS.

A SPRINKLE ON THE CROWN
WORKS WONDERS
ON:
HEADACHES
DEPRESSION
AILING LIBIDO.

DEAD INSIDE?
WOMEN'S TEARS
MAKE YOUR INTERIORS
SPARKLE.

DON'T SETTLE
FOR CHEAP ALTERNATIVES
LIKE FRETTING
OR GRIEVING.

100% WOMEN'S TEARS
ARE BOTTLED FRESH
AT THE KITCHEN SINK
WITH GOOD
OLD FASHIONED LOVE

JUST LIKE MOTHER
USED TO MAKE.

The Strikes

It strikes me out of nowhere
and again I'm stricken
by it – it glances off my sunglasses
it strikes me for the first time
again on the head
dazed by the backhanded blessing

I'm alive to it, I'm dumbstruck
going Dumb – dumb – dummy!
Feeling the sensation fading
I strike myself because I have to
keep my eyes open to let the sun in
and then I realise I was struck
by myself from the beginning

Still the striking goes on
whether awake or asleep I'm there
slapstick and deadpan smacked
by a skillet to the back of the head
going Gong! Gong! Gong!
Filling the auditorium inside
with laughter canned before I was born

What is Wrong With Me

I'm completely helpless.
I can't even turn off the light
and open the blinds.
I just lie here, trembling
at the vibration of the works
down on the corner.

My mood has collapsed,
and, once again, I don't
understand: it was a good day.
I woke late, and in my time,
drifted down to Hurstbridge.
I had coffee and cake,
fed the chooks some oats.
The rain even stopped.

And the call finally came:
I've found somewhere else,
another place to live.
I used to feel at home
sleeping on the desert floor,
alone beneath the stars.
At sunrise I'd shake down
the dust – it was nothing.

Now my arms and legs ache.
I don't have the energy to cry.
And it's turned sunny now,
and blue – and here am I
hiding in my childhood room,
from my mum's questions
and my father's eyes.

King Tide

We woke up in the middle of a king tide,
a slow yet joyous creeping of water,
bathed in moonlight. We laughed
once we realized what was happening –
a thing neither of us had experienced
before we were wallowing in it.
We had our tent in the branches quickly.

I feel that I remember
the water touching our feet.

I climbed up to your loft in the warehouse,
and said, "I'm going, you want to come?"
You thought I was talking about
going down the road for a pack of smokes.
We hitched around half the continent.

I cannot say when morphine found us,
but it must have been after that night.
Drugs followed us wherever we went;
pursued us all the way to Darwin.

I don't blame you for letting me go;
some things are bigger than us.
Who understands the way things move?
All I know is that we were touched,
and we had to make do.

Pacific Ocean

I held my breath
for several years,
descended
to a soundless place
touched only
by soft light.

On the surface,
my skin boiled up
into hives.
The doctor
he ran his fingers
over the lumps,
but misread me.
"An allergy to
something," he said.
I couldn't call out,
not from that place.
It never occurred
to me, anyway –
I was swimming
with seahorses,
rainbowfish, squid,
building a castle
with a moat
and drawbridge.

Boxing Day

I don't want to write poetry.
I don't want to watch cricket.
Walking would be okay, except
I don't want it.
I don't want to
talk on the phone,
watch Netflix,
eat Guylian shells.

A picnic at the reservoir –
now there is something that
I really don't want.
I don't want J.B. vouchers,
Westfield vouchers, Hoyt's.
And don't even bother about
getting me a card.

What I want
no one can give me today.

I don't know what else
I don't want right now,
but I'm sure that I'll know it
when I see it.

III

Peninsula

Each day as I drive to Rosebud,
I watch the pelicans
far above, pointing the way
to the ocean or the other shore.
They're heading inland now,
high on sunshine and warmth.

One eye on the road ahead,
one to where the blue goes –
I know I'm not a good driver.
There is a terrible beauty
to their silent progress.

But when they start to circle,
my heart clenches like a brake.
I don't know how I got here,
I just washed up on the shore.
Wherever I go I am a tourist,
and my body carries such weight.

Moon-age Daydream

The church of mad love
is such a holy place to be
- David Bowie

1.

Let's be the best
of ourselves – the birds
are fetching twigs like
there's no tomorrow.

Sit by the river
on a blanket for two.
We are needed here,
don't you know –
it wouldn't be spring
without us.

2.

In a deep waking sleep,
my eyes search my mind.
I can see the wind,
I understand the trees
and how they are moved,
so violent and green.

As you shine through,
my words are absorbed
into the page.

3.

I said, "Let's get married
and settle down in the bush.
We'll have koalas; we can
push them around in prams."
She said, "We'll have to separate
the males from the females
so they don't rape one another."

4.

I guess I'm still manic –
I woke up too excited.
I said to my parents,
this is not right, it's 9 am
and I'm happy to see you.

5.

I don't love your singing.
I am completely unmoved
by the karaoke you post
on my Facebook wall.
I don't care at all
for your glitter lipstick –
and I should do I know.

Your body frightens me.
It's just too much, I can't
take care of it all.
To reveal everything
to a stranger like that –
I'm just too fragile.
I was only diagnosed
last week, you know.

6.

What is happening to me?
I don't understand –
I used to be over there
where at least I knew
who I was in all this.

Now I'm the other guy,
on a hilltop, voiceless.
The sun bobs up again,
flowers open their eyes.

7.

Dark and light chase each
other across the earth
forever – how are we
supposed to feel in all that?

8.

She clutches the truth
and the way in her hands,
stands on the mountain,
hair blowing like
she's in an 80s video.

She sends me YouTube clips
with titles like "The truth
about kinetic energies
the world powers
don't want you to know."

9.

She found me by magic.
Like attracts like,
and I wrote on Facebook
about the change happening
inside of me, my feet
so far off the ground.

But I wanted to feel
something with her,
I wanted to feel
good. I implied strongly
I might just love her.
I think I did – did I?

Visions

I'm climbing this hill,
though I have to say
I'm hardly present
for anything right now.
I'm in between places,
and I'm tired.

I've been too many people
   too many times.

I was in the gay scene
when I was sweet sixteen,
but I wasn't really gay.
I was a goth by '88,
but suicidal girlfriends
are a drag.

Nothing's that simple.
I was a little bit gay,
and kind of dead already.

When I became an addict,
everything was compressed
into a singular darkness.
But it couldn't last.
I'd worn all my clothes out.

Now I'm this house sitter
guy who lives a pastoral life.
      I slop the hen
      I hug alpacas
      I stare down the setting sun.

I'm someone else's dream,
but I'm climbing this hill.

And as I climb, I see
the fields stretch out,
blank and silent.
I sketch a whippet
nearby, on a string.
He drags a slender woman,
bare-footed, in slacks.
I block in a BBQ
and a stooped figure
with a spatula.

I add a stick family,
playing badminton.
The wind is alive now,
twigs and branches
cartwheel by.

I'm not very good
at this sort of thing,
but I will try now
to draw myself
into the picture.

Airborne

I want to go
in a hot air balloon.
We don't have to
have sex in the balloon,
but I want to go
in a hot air balloon
with you.

And you can of course
remain my ex.
For all the hot air,
the bodies rising,
there's no need to fear
the landing.
The whole device
is a parachute.

Strange Calling

Pissing in nature
is one of man's great pleasures.
It's something that happens
and happens again, the more
that you're in the elements.

It only seems more natural
as the years go by, until the flow
of the whole experience
is not unlike the currents
that the eagle glides upon,
the great tides of an estuary,
or the way the birds respond
to the gathering night.

Those off-track moments
have become a private place
that return to you often.
After the day has been spent
writing about marble tiles,
you close your eyes for a moment
in traffic, on the way home.

You're earthing water
in a forest you cannot name –
or it may be a confluence of places:
the camp at Murrindindi maybe,
that walk down to Cascade Falls.

All-Nighter

As time grinds on,
I have less tolerance
for emotional pain,
and less understanding
of what it means.
I feel trapped in my life.
I don't enjoy anything.
I don't like who I am.

There was a time
when drink and drugs
were the best I could do.
I didn't want to die,
but I didn't want to live
either.

It's not a drug problem
at the moment,
it's a sickness of the soul,
manifesting as
sarcastic parents,
suspicious security guards,
lorikeets in the rain.

I'm calling now
on everyone I know,
on God and
the idea of sunshine.
I am waiting
for your presence
above the lake,

or a maybe breath of air
passing through
at the 24 hr Kmart.

Funeral Party

The reception's nibblies
hide in a corner of the room.
I go over to introduce myself,
but they're in a terrible state.

I'm so sorry I dive into the M&Ms
and wallow for pity's sakes,
what's wrong with me, ooh,
lookee-lookee, a blue one.

Meanwhile everyone's over there,
where the Cheezels aren't,
where people have something else
– I can't say, because Cheezels,

Cheezels in an inextinguishable
jumbo pack of elsewhere.

And these so-called people
are apparently in relation to me –
they make eye contact,
have opinions and jobs.

But I have a Cheezel halo,
I have M&Ms for eyes.
I'm suited up, pale-skinned
and sweating like a candle.

He died in an M&M cave-in,
the humble stone will read,
a landslide of polite,
his mouth a graveyard gate.

The Circle Will Not Be Broken

The circle will not be broken
whether my shadow is long or short.
And, really, I could be one of those
kangaroo shapes on the hill,
or a leaf on the candle-bark tree.

Please don't try to find me.
I have gone to be with the trees
and the grasses and dirt,
where I may be dispersed.

Classify me as fauna,
take away my name.
I've always been a missing person.
I roll over with the earth.

What time takes from you
it will give to me.

Glow Worms

I regret that we didn't see
the glow worms together.

Like always, we were poor
time and money-wise.
Our desperate little holidays.
Later you said you wished
that we had never gone away.
Forcing what should be easy,
it's no holiday – yes, I know,
you're right. But now
I wish we had gone there.

We had too many brochures,
and held them to feel
their weight: The Otway Fly,
Loch Ard Gorge, the Apostles
by helicopter. But you returned
to Kennett River Glow Worms,
an A4 photocopy, all text.
Standing in the summer sun,
I just couldn't see it.
I don't know why I took control.
I needed – what did I need? –
Something I could take back
to Coburg.

The years have passed on.

I've never seen the glow worms,
but I still think about them
sometimes, when it's late
and I'm lying in my bed.
They shine for me in the dark,
and I gaze up at them,
my whole body a kind of wish.
But I can't really see them.
I wish that we had gone there.
We needed a different light.

Caution

Objects in the rear-view mirror
may appear closer than they really are.
A car crash, for example,
or your parents waving goodbye.
Even as you accelerate, you will find
it's all there, framed in your mirror.

When something looms large –
say you're pursued by an ambulance,
the siren high, headlights flashing –
you need to let it pass by if you can,
but the important thing is not to look.
That's how accidents happen.

At night, if the mirror's a bit askew,
you may seem to catch the ghost
of yourself. A strange reflection:
your disembodied eyes seem to float
and shudder along with the car.

Take no more than a glance.
Whatever you do, don't be afraid.

Terminus

in memory of Brownie

When I saw you stumble
for the first time
I began to understand
the stations
of the cross.

But at Footscray Station
on the way to the vet's
when the V/Line blew its horn
and you stopped breathing

and I stared at you
upturned and shining
like a crescent moon

for a moment
I saw heaven and hell
hold hands
forming a perfect circle of Tao

and through both sides
– shining –
your wide-open eyes.

There There

The way I feel
the colour of blue
the wind raking everything
no not that

The birds I hear
but never see
the vineyard the fence
the sound of cars
the person who pissed
on this bench

Yes and no and okay
day and night
saplings mountains
you said but truth
I said metaphor blah
blah feeling ideas

The wind the dirt
walking eyes closed
my breath my hand
I imagined something more
but my breath
my breath and my hand

Highpoint Lowes

At 40 I've reached a place
where nothing seems to fit me.

Kmart and Target
keep a few one-size-fits-all
garments on the racks
for people like me,
not that we're important
economically.
Lakers t-shirts, cargo shorts.

I've come so far
to reach this point.
The front of store stuff
at Lowes is on sale –
$20 jeans, $15 trousers,
and polo necks for $10.
I go to the trousers.

There are all the colours:
cream, olive, tan.
I'm considering navy,
because I could act like
I had to wear them
for some kind of job.

An assistant comes over;
there's a middle-aged
motherliness about her
that I always found repellent.
Now I find it attractive.

"Can I help you?" she says.
I look down at my denim jeans,
t-shirt and man boobs.
She doesn't seem to notice
my complete despair.

"We don't have the greatest
range in our stores,
but I'm sure we can find
something to suit you."

All I can think is that
she would suit me.
I would get up of a morning
and look in the mirror
and see her still asleep
over my shoulder and think,
"You don't look
too bad there, buddy."

But she's loaded me up
with trousers, shirts,
jeans stiff as cardboard.

The changeroom is tiny
and there's nothing inside –
no wrapping, no discards,
and nowhere to sit.

As I shake myself free
of my loose garments,
I see my body in the mirror:
it's like an outfit belonging
to someone else.

The clothes I'm holding
are heavy. If I could be
anywhere but where I am
I'd already be there.

But I have no choice,
I've worn out my clothes.
Besides, I'm here already,
in the changing room.
It's time to get busy.

June is On Fire

for June Torcasio

Someone stoked the coke burner
under her desk today, until
all the muses were smoked out
into the open.

And so it begins: she fixes you
with those eyes, that grin.
She's stoked by something,
that's for sure.

Her desk is starting to blister,
her hair erupts in flames.
Electrical charges leap
across her cranial hemispheres;
wherever she turns her eyes,
spot fires appear.

Embers leap ahead now,
burning down boring houses.
Her eyes are two angry suns.
"Look out, look out!"
the townsfolk are yelling –
"June is on fire!"

My Acoustic Guitar

My acoustic guitar lies across the bed.
It may not have that classical figure,
but it makes for a comfortable shape.
The reddish stain on the back of the neck
brings out the grain, like strands of hot toffee
that run down right to the tuning pegs.

The top is made of a bright spruce,
But, with the blinds open, it has taken on
some of the winter hues.
The grain is straight and fine, for the most part,
but is interrupted by crazy rivulets,
that shimmer like an alluvial creek.
The effect can at times seem like static,
a current running across the guitar.
At other times it is a scar, a reminder that the wood
once had another meaningful life.

The life we share now is strange and far away.
Both of us are twisted into shapes
that are beautiful in a certain light,
and together we make something
that lives in the air for only a moment,
each note living and dying for each other.

Tourist Information

If you want
a view of the mountains
the best view
is from down here.

Don't bother
climbing them.
All you'll see
is tree after tree
after tree.

My Bird

I want you to take
the lorikeets with you.
I only ask that
you unlock that cage.

Take them to a quiet place
by the river, or a hill
somewhere nearby.

Swing the gates wide.

Hear their crazy chimes,
see their flights of colour
into the waiting arms
of the trees.

I want you to know
you need never feel alone.
You can always find them,
if you just stop to listen
and open that cage.

Meditation

Breathe in the open fields,
breathe out Mum and Dad.
Breathe in lorikeets,
breathe out Andrew O'Keefe.
Hold that out breath.

Follow the river now.
Let notions of time drift.

You're not forty-nine
and living with his parents,
you're a twinkling light.
You're not an NA member
on a disability pension,
you're an unfurling frond.

Wait until you are really alone.
Remove your mask.
You are the wombat hole,
      the mosquito,
      the tadpole.

Inhale golden sunshine.
Fart out VicRoads hold music.

Hello, Cocky

Might I gesture now
to the corellas in the tree?

Would that I could
bring your mind to rest
on the question
of the cocky's crest.

If you look you may find
yourself eye to eye
with a peckish turtledove.
Gazing at the lake
long enough,
you may find a cormorant
comes bobbing up.

In the season of spring
you may very well see
a sparrow zip past
carrying a sprig.

What more can I do
than introduce you:
bird, reader – reader, bird.

www.ingramcontent.com/pod-product-compliance
Lightning Source LLC
Chambersburg PA
CBHW070042030726
47506CB00003B/836